STEVE LEVINE

To and For

NEW AND SELECTED POEMS

COFFEE HOUSE PRESS :: MINNEAPOLIS :: 1992

The author wishes to acknowledge the following publications, in which some of these poems have appeared: *Batteria, Beyond Baroque Magazine, Bingo, joe soap's canoe, Mag City, New Observations, Nice to See You, Oink!, Out of This World: An Anthology of the St. Mark's Poetry Project, Poetry Project Newsletter, Teachers & Writers, Transfer,* and *The World.*

Thanks go to Jerome Foundation; Minnesota State Arts Board; the National Endowment for the Arts, a federal agency; and Northwest Area Foundation for support of this project.

Coffee House Press books are available to bookstores through our primary distributor, Consortium Book Sales & Distribution, 287 E. Sixth St., Suite 365, St. Paul, Minnesota 55101. Our books are also available through all major library distributors and jobbers, and through most small press distributors, including Bookpeople, Bookslinger, Inland, and Small Press Distribution. For personal orders, catalogs or other information, write to:
Coffee House Press
27 North Fourth Street, Suite 400, Minneapolis, MN 55401

Library of Congress Cataloging-in-Publication Data

Levine, Steve, 1953-
        To and for : new and selected poems / by Steve Levine.
        p. cm.
        ISBN 0-918273-71-4 : $10.95
        I. Title.
PS3562.E913T6 1992
811'.54--DC20   92-3245
                                CIP

Contents

for Jeff Levine

Selected Poems

Epistle

You are my friend, no compendium
     of singular devotion
Your book is here with me
Sitting on the sofa, golden
Sunlight streaming in
Like the electric voice of a calm commander
You've been to all the scenic places
What a beautiful life!

Who knows who you are? Seven
Wise guys in Greece?
Where did Confucius live?

When the Lone Ranger goes over there
     to get those eight pigeons
I'd gladly give you up who'd give
     me up so easily, but you don't
     give up, so easily you're
Up on my calendar, there

Colder weather warmer clothes enter
Great flocks of black coats cut out
     under the trees, dash
     in your big machine
     in your big depot
     the brain . . .

          SILENCE . . .

Who is as eloquent as you? Nobody
     is as eloquent as you, that is you
          that is a person

3

One middle-aged dame of swarthy complexion w/earrings
    as big as after-dinner coffee cups could not
    play the original. Glaucous magnolia

Exquisite Indian, sailboat in the snow, in flexible
    equilibrium all soldier, all poet, all scholar, all
    saint, all some one gift or meritorious success, one tough
    gazooka which loves all palookas, harmonious human multitude!

The Best of Friends

Besides Vincenzo (renamed James), and
Salvatore (later Frank), Alphonse, Amadeo
Ermino (later John and nicknamed Mimi), Umberto
(Albert John), Matthew, Nick, Mafalda, and Rose,
The Five Points, the Plug-Uglies, the Dead Rabbits
Confirmed them in their tribalism.

Mister Terranova, Artichoke King,
Lupo the Wolf, pathological killer,
The apelike Monk Eastman, the aromatic
Biff, a tall slim jim named Mae, would go
The limit for Johnny, and Big Jim Colosimo.

Bunny Hug, Pretty Boy, Dardanella, Yacki, Hacki,
Wicki, Wacki, Woo, Oakie, Arkie, and Mizoo rubbing elbows
With "Lovin' Putty," Mike de Pike Merchant of Vice
Who looked like a Surinam toad, wizened confederate
Izzy the Rat, Hinky Dink, Bathhouse John (who worked
As a rubber in a Turkish bath), and Dion,
To whose protection Jim owed his rise.

Big Jim, bulky person festooned with stones, precious
Blue elephants or horses on several fingers, on his belt,
Suspender, garter buckle, tiepin, on his fob, shirt
Bosom, cuffs and vest, he fastened a sunburst, hair gleaming
Onyx, agate eyes (note chipped state of the rim)
Whose revivification translated cultic citations,
Alluded to numerous incantations, either held in hand
Or set on a stand, greenish calcite or aragonite, Big Jim

And operatic Luisa Tetrazinni shaking hands, "Welcome
To Arnold's Homeopathic Lunch, Blubber Bob Gray,
Madame Therese, Alice Fly, Nell Bly, Alkali, and Black May"

A few doors to the south, the House of All Nations

French Emma, Sappho, English Ada and Minna Everliegh
Married brothers who maltreated them, tiny spasms of awe
And humor carried them away in the mobile joys of joyous urgency
In the Copper Room, in the Moorish Room, in the Turkish Room,
In the Chinese, Egyptian, and Japanese rooms heavy
With incense, paphians, the Vice Commission, a
Newsboy and a bootblack, a green jackass, a red bull
On the bed, a nude bearded hero punted by a prow, that shadow
Savonarola, a long litany of Latin poets, everybody
There was there, the best of friends

Modern Science

I put my heart on a wire
Tug it
Send it off
Chicago to California
It sees lots of wondrous sights
In the interval along the way

For instance, it sees the florescent flatlands
    of the bizarre but tastefully
    exotic Midwest, where
    chrome is grown
It is astonished
By this marvel of La Science Moderne

The Plains are truly plain in comparison

Though it, my heart, is not surprised
To see the exploding Indians
    of the Plains.
But now I think it's gone too far

My heart, going the wrong way
Get back here, muscle!

I unhook it, wrench it
Inside out, hook it up anew, and . . .
It goes on its groove back down the wire
Through high blue gray green
It can be seen heading southwest

My heart. It is real red
And pumping like a motherfucker!
But it's nothing like a cock.
It's a red heart
It's a red running heart
It's a red heart running out
        of Arizona.
I put it on a wire
Tugged it
To make sure
Sent it off
From Chicago to California.
It's very big
To see you, and happy
After its trip and many exciting adventures

Seconds

A mackerel sky

                  masses

       small

   rounded, high   detached,

        lots of

           Blue sky in the gaps;

    Oozes

        gutsy : gusty

            motile
             pillows

          w/pearly domes & steeples

              *

Whooshing   sounds   loud . . .
                          high up.

              *

        This natural occlusion stuff

         was the bunk,

Duenna, Guardian Angel,
Counselor, Hygienist, Mid-
Wife, Governess, Den Mom, Caring
Friend,

where we bunked
down
in the aerie
above the woe—
lined streets.

*

Your language, visible   Suspended, in air

A cloudy clump of hair   Springing into an *o*

for
seconds

A Gothic Gesture

Is this the movie in which James Mason
Slams his cane down on Ann Todd's fingers?

Because she is playing piano? Yes, it was
A gothic gesture and made Mason a matinee idol

Overnight. One night, nights
Passed, we see him first

Meditating on a record by the Troggs, then groggy
Putting his fist through the ballroom window

In a sudden froglike fit of angst, his features
A concentrated form of melancholy, green . . .

Green and lumpy landscaping, brooding
Piano, parodistic weltschmerz.

June

wash my hands with Lava

feel nothing & be

primitive, proud

alternate

      sit down then walk

hoedown with a shoulder holster

talk about nothing   itch

talk about invention

                   iron pants

love the way you dry your hair

babble   stop

read Reverdy in the stifling heart

The Chamber I Inhabit Is Finally Cleared

Beautiful weather
Just "beautiful"
Just the way you say "simply"

Is there a term, meaning a time
more beautiful? No. Doubt it.
Beautiful weather. Wonderment. Leaves like rust.

Wonderful crow fall in the yard making metal noisy
as they drift into the chain-link
fence. Blam! Beautiful ether.

I walked home and collapsed on the bed
I walked home
I walked home collapsed

On the bed, beautiful weather.
On the way home I heard a couple of heels scrapping
behind me. Beautiful wonderment of weather.

Along the concrete
I heard two heels scrapping.
I heard scraping, collapsing on the bed, behind me

I think it was the springs.
They, no doubt, are beautiful, touching, tired.
A persistent noise has followed me home.

Shit! This persistent noise has followed me home.
Crow metal beautiful link the scrape. Rust,
is there a term more beautiful?

Luscious

That's the way
they paint them
in France
        tucked up
        aprons full
of peas in pods, on occasion
bursting forth
with green kinetic
energy.

        The master
painter Édouard
Vuillard
loved peas
overwhelmingly,
but was discreet
in his passion.

Although hectic
multitudes of podded peas
shoot throughout his placid
masterpi

I alone know of this.

Because
he told me

He was my
father

In fact,
it showed.
All over his face.

Huskies

The husky is one
of the most rugged animals
alive. It can survive temper-
atures that plunge far below
0 in winds of 100 miles per hour
or more. Huskies have instincts
that reach back for thousands
of years, avoiding hidden breaks
in the ice, picking up old trails,
and finding the way home in all
but the wildest of weather. When
a young call girl staggers into
the squad room and falls dead
muttering "He's going to kill
my mama," the husky sets out
to discover just who *he* is.

Poem

When
that black
woman walking
with the black
coat white scarf
casually arranged
one large loop
ends
swept back
& down her back
a tremendous white
safety pin set
against a toddling
patch of black on black
lets go, her pony
sized naturally
white curly hair
poodle tears off
into the open
field opposite
the Kosminsky elementary
school

Outer Limits

Entomologist Ben Fields
was experimenting with bees—
and now they are going to
experiment with him

Little Feat

Insects
& their noises
rise

in waves
& sing
along

the high-
way
Hoy, Hoy, Hoy

Homage to Kurt Schwitters

Woo it
chew it
tinny who

shoe it
stew it
tinny who

I grew it I
knew it
blew
it too, tinny who

who you who you who

is the music
of the tinny
tinny who

we keep it
here in our shoe, our
glorious shoe

holds our
tinny
who

who
knows
what songs

it will sing
tonight
to you

only the tinny
tin tin tiny
tinny who

tinny woh
tinny ho
tinny who

tinny
who tinny
who tinny who

Poem

Red fit Zen
you sock me in
a lib gap hem

a fizz pit dock
of beans in the quiet
moola ear

where eons vie
an aero quim tie
bug wise hock laps

on Viet anus you
imagine a Fudd
lobe wreck

the synap feuds
that imbue a geo
virile ack ow

and fuel doer naps
that hoot wax
and gack bum nine

as odors pan
umbilica kin hugs
to vex eye awe

and doors bulge
mica nike toes
wan pixy ha

and vulgar
Ike canoes fume
timid neon hobo yap

the lugar pablum
of meant nose ode
yikes

to rage Lulu meat
and hose open
the wok fib

you mope snooze
ululate the gam
fever jinx

you OK phobic zoos
amble the geek
detour avenues

as Bambi eek
ooze huns lope
avid doggie rot

ascend with zonk
hue palm goo
eeiioouuuu

and eiaaaooooo
O oxy fog trancs
wobble end up

in your kupf
bellows of ovum
tinge a feral daze!

The Cycles of Heaven

*Writers, I Believe, Should Establish a Firm Home Base,
Get to Know Themselves and Their Neighbors, Govern Themselves
By the Rules of Their Community While Rejecting Its
Provincialities and Prejudices, and, in General, Try To
Live Down the Byronic-Bohemian Tradition*

An American Tragedy

*Two bicycles—one female model, one male model—face each other,
front wheel to front wheel. The bikes form a V-shape, the exterior
angle of which faces the audience. Otherwise the stage is empty,
bathed in total darkness.*

(One female and one male voice, in unison, from offstage)

THE CYCLES OF HEAVEN!

*(Red and blue spotlights come up on the bicycles. For the duration of
the play, white light comes up very slowly—so that it takes the entire
script for the white light to be fully lit.)*

FEMALE: Omaha Omaha Omaha
          Omaha Omaha Omaha
          Omaha

MALE: Omaha Omaha Omaha
        Omaha Omaha Omaha
        Omaha

UNISON: Omaha Omaha Omaha
          Omaha Omaha Omaha
          Omaha

MALE &
FEMALE: *(Spoken in round style, twice)*
            I just couldn't stand
            that hysteric sound
            coming down on me—
            I was no big talker
            Seemingly rather
            Withdrawn, I wasn't
            Married, and had no
            Children, I believed
            Something, it was
            Worrying me all the time.
            When I am not writing
            I'm drinking, smoking,
            Taking, and vice versa.

FEMALE: Can you say Omaha?

MALE: Omawah.

UNISON: Omaha; THE CYCLES OF HEAVEN,
         An American Tragedy.

MALE: Big stars are snapping
       Outside Omaha, their
       Interiors limitless
       As my great emptiness.

FEMALE: Omaha Omaha Omaha
Omaha Omaha Omaha
Omaha

THE CYCLES OF HEAVEN.

MALE: Ten minutes before
Time began, ten minutes
Was maybe an hour. . . .

UNISON: Omaha!

FEMALE: *(Fingersnap)*
Who dies?

MALE: *(Fingersnap)*
Who doesn't?

FEMALE: Can you say Omawah?

MALE: Omaha Omaha Omaha
Omaha Omaha Omaha
Omaha

THE CYCLES OF HEAVEN: An American Tragedy.

FEMALE: A writer, I believe, should establish a firm home
Base, get to know herself and her neighbors, govern
Herself by the rules of her community while rejecting
Its provincialities and prejudices, and, in general, try
To live down the Byronic-Bohemian tradition.

MALE: A writer, I believe, should establish a firm home
Base, get to know himself and his neighbors, govern
Himself by the rules of his community while rejecting
Its provincialities and prejudices, and, in general, try
To live down the Byronic-Bohemian tradition.

UNISON: Omawah Omawah Omawah
Omawah Omawah Omawah
Omawah

FEMALE: What we have here
Is a pocket of autonomy
Statues toppled
In the rapture of greenery. . . .

MALE: Big stars are snapping outside
Their interiors limitless
As my great emptiness. . . .

FEMALE: Spring's sudden flush
The annual contractions
of a nerve-
Lined, thin-rimmed flower!

UNISON: THE CYCLES OF HEAVEN!

> Writers, we believe, should establish a firm home
> Base, get to know themselves and their neighbors, govern
> Themselves by the rules of their community while rejecting
> Its provincialities and prejudices, and, in general, try
> To live down the Byronic-Bohemian tradition.

UNISON: Omaha Omaha Omaha
          Omaha Omaha Omaha
               Omaha

MALE: I just can't stand
      that hysteric sound
      Coming down on me!
      I hate prettiness!
      I hate the signs
      Of the zodiac!
      I am no big talker
      I am not married
      I have no children
      I believe something
      It is worrying me
      When I am not writing
      I'm drinking, smoking,
      Taking, and vice versa.

FEMALE: Omaha, can you say Omaha?

MALE: Omawah.

THE END

New Poems

Poem

Now stop that
sort of
stilted talk

Get more serious
minded
about your work

And let your words
make trees
walk like giant

capital *T*s
straight
out of the forest

Clear Water

Clear water
waiting, waits
to fill the once
full San Pellegrino
Pre-Alp (Italiano)
mineral water bottle,
and to swirl. Clearly,
the water is waiting—
it waits to fill it
greenly as the bottle
is not so strangely
green and intended
for those two new
cut Dutch tulips.
Once they are put
there, clear water
waiting to swirl up
swirls up though just
a few beads enough
to slip the green

bottle lip, and all

of this is meant to sit

all motion, composed, over

there before a print of

Johannes Vermeer's *Officer and*

Laughing Girl.

Lost Dog

Three legs blind
in right eye

Little left
ear long gone

Castrated
recently

Answers to the name of
"Lucky"

Do Animals Think?

Yes, they do.
But not of you.

Forgetting

I'm forgetting

I'm human

Some Philosophical Thoughts

Astronomy, yes

Botany, yes

Philosophy, no

Little Cards

Little Cards

Pascal and
Descartes

God Is Dead

Good

Good God

An old
story

An Old Story

Good God Almighty!
waileth Jerry Lee

Mr. Lewis

Jerry or Jerry Lee
It's all the same to me

They Met

And blended into one
another

The "Killer" plus the "Comic"

Are a part of our popular cultural heritage
now

Like Dark Music

I hear it, see
it as well

As Well

You might
as well

Turn Inward

We turn inward
and it is good

It

Couldn't be beat

I Might Miss a Beat

Or it might
miss me

Poem

The Reading Is Shitty

Reader on Ex-Lax?

Impure Forms

Imperfected for you

Things That Are Suspended

Take on weight, wait

Slow in Coming

Then not

Stretch My Legs

Please

Honoring Past Members

Members, you know, members

A Silver Honda

I'll be getting on

What's Shaking?

What isn't?

Flux

The essence of existence

Heraclitus

Felt that

And Plunged

Into such a rich mind

Miserable Life

To climb the stairs with
        slippers,
To slip off with every step.
        To feel
One's foot slipping, or to
        not to.
To put one's foot, then,
        (an
Accident) into the one
        wet mud
Rut (and splatter the one
        woman you
Love). And at the theater
        to shove to
Slip in, just to sit behind
        a Giant.
And, also, at the moment
        your most
Grandiose train of thought
        is pulling
Out, to know your close
        friend
Is dead; and then, again,
        to go on.
Ted, in the dead of winter,
        to spread cold
Butter on soft bread, to go on
        to eat one's
Daily tiny eggs in order. . . .
        Then, when one

Must fish life's wet bar of soap
        out from under
Some furniture, to find it covered
        with horrific hair
Of cat, fur, and feathers. To do
        this. To do
That. To do this. To do that.
        This is not at
All amusing! Miserable life!

A Calendar

These days
Days fly
Really, by . . .

Slips
The mind
To rip

Each
Month's
Page

Off.
O
Tiny

Diurnal
Windows,
You are

Stiff
Competition
For art.

To My Father

The un-
broachable

time we
discovered,

you move
over. So long

Dad, so long . . .

To My Father

Dad, there
is a tavern

in this town,
its contents

often spin
around ...

The Wall Is Better

With one eye
I read a book

with the other
eye I watch the

wall; sometimes
the wall is better.

The Mountain

Why does the
mountain rise

to meet my
feet? Because

I set myself
down on it.

Heading North

The family that eats
together eats together

eats together and eats
together, rides a

tiny Honda together,
two of them, huge

matching bellies
heading north

Appleton, Wisconsin

In what is called
the Paper Valley

I ate an Aryan
sub-sandwich

dubbed "Sausage
hoagie." Also

ingested: Germanic egg
foo young-like chop suey

mit Minute Rice
und heavy beef gravy.

Red Snowflake

Drops on my tongue

Summer

Fry in the ointment

The Six Don'ts

The six don'ts don't
don't don't don't
don't don't

Ode to Navanax Inermis

O rat-size

yellow-dotted

brown-and-blue

hermaphroditic slug of the sea!

Your male genitalia bob freely

on the right side

of your head and

a few inches be-

hind one finds

a slit opening

to the ovary.

And although

with your round

single-foot flap

of sensitive skin

wrapped about your

tubular body you

resemble an un-

dulating enchilada,

you are not flexible

enough to have sex

with yourself.

O *Navanax*
inermis, if
you can't do
it with your-
self, just what
is the point in
being a slug?

In the Text

of this slight
poem I feel com-
pelled to tell you
that in (what I take
to be) a relatively
obscure Clint Eastwood
vehicle (a movie) called
Joe Kidd Clint the Joe
Kidd of said title
does single-handedly
thwart the violent force
Robert Duvall's raging
megalomania, etc., and
in the process save
the former lover of
one (Juan?) Chavez
the deprived of his
land Mexican-American
peasant revolutionary
from the filthy (I have
to use that word) filthy
grip of the stereotypic
white fascist enterprising
bastard just to tell her
maybe one or two hours
later that he did not
(repeat he did not)
accomplish this near-
superhuman feat solely
to save her life. "I
did not accomplish this

near-superhuman feat sole-
ly to save your life. . . ."
(now I'm paraphrasing Joe)
"It's just that I actually I
uh really admire your politics."

The Ballad of Laszlo Toth

With five or six
well-placed blows

he knocked off
the marble virgin's nose

Love Poem

Your mind is like a poet's mind
Active and aware

Freckles are your bared neck's necklace
Random, ravishing

Naturally occurring
Quick thinking and encircling

Deep haphazard beauty—
That's your poetry

Lisa Reed   533-3223

She

tried to liken me
to James Joyce, re

his vanity (sartorial)
his passionate thing

for tiny Italian
fine leather shoes—

pointy silly
very large girl.

Surprise

Vivian is a lesbian

Poem

As the subway pitches
Into the tunnel, she appears!
Mirrored in the black window

Gina

sniffs the cut and dried
long dead eucalyptus
says it smells "So wonderful!"

Reading

In the binding of the Basho
I kept for my own
One of your long hairs

For K. M.

I am going to sit here for about one minute
Dedicated to you the air all soft breezes
Lost in the lofty green branches

Contempt

I feel it rising within me—
That which made great lizards rise
To the trees and now with wings, sing
Sweet songs of withering derision.

Poem

Good morning you will be loved
On this glorious day
You will be hated, both
Kissed and despised. Good
Morning bright steps rising
To brown stone buildings
Colorful individuals angling
Down them toward the train—
Sadly heedlessly or in inspired
Reckless ecstasy on this glorious
Day you will love you will hate both
Kiss and despise. The grotesque beauty
The radiantly ugly the genius or the just
Plain foolish and goofy, good morning
All! On this glorious day the boundless
White beret is on your lovely heads go ahead
Love and be loved hate and be hated kiss
and despise be kissed and despised!